# How I Survived My Borderline Girlfriend

## The Only Thing That Cures Narcissistic Abuse

### By

### Michael William Denney

*YouTube Channel*

***"The ONE Thing That Heals BPD and NPD Abuse"***

Disclaimer
3

Introduction
6

Your Relationship Is Not What You Think It Is
13

What Happened? Why Did She Change?
21

Your Borderline Is Not Rational
35

Your Borderline Doesn't Know You Exist
42

Why Your Borderline Girlfriend "Splits"
54

Is Your Borderline Girlfriend Evil?
73

Why You Can't Accept Your Borderline Is Mentally Ill
83

The ONE Thing That Heals BPD and NPD Abuse
92

# Disclaimer

This book is not meant to diagnose treat or cure any type of emotional or mental illness. If you believe you suffer from or know anyone whom you believe suffers from any kind of emotional, mental or psychological disorder, please contact a mental health professional.

This book is only meant as information to help understand the experience a person may have as a result of having a romantic relationship with someone who suffers from untreated and/or undiagnosed borderline personality disorder or narcissistic personality disorder or is co-morbid with both disorders.

This book is not meant to be read by people who currently suffer from BPD or NPD. This book is meant as a source of information and entertainment for non-disordered people who are currently in or have been in a romantic relationship with someone with undiagnosed and/or untreated BPD or NPD.

If someone who is currently in treatment for BPD or NPD chooses to read this book, it is my suggestion that such a person only read this book with the intention of understanding the experience of the non-disordered partner in such a relationship.

The description of the experience of a non-disordered partner of the motives and emotions of a pwBPD may not be accurately reflecting the clinical understanding of the pathology of BPD. I am just describing what BPD looks like and feels like to the partner of a disordered person.

Whatever conclusions or descriptions are used by the writer to express the appearance of BPD in romantic relationships is only for understanding the experience of the partner, not to accurately describe the mental illness of BPD from a clinical perspective.

If you want to know what BPD is from the perspective of the science of psychology, please seek out sources of information by psychologists and psychiatrists.

BPD is a very serious but treatable mental illness that should only be diagnosed by a qualified mental health professional. Anyone who believes they might be suffering from BPD should seek out a qualified psychologist for treatment.

Any suggestions made by the author to the non-disordered partner are just that: a layman's suggestion. Any action a person chooses to take to alleviate any experience of trauma from having been in a relationship with a person with BPD is solely the responsibility of the reader.

The author takes no responsibility for the actions taken by any reader of this book. All readers are encouraged to seek out qualified mental and psychological treatment for any emotional trauma they believe they might have endured.

# Introduction

There are no shortage of resources for people with borderline personality disorder to find help for their condition. But, as I personally discovered, there are very few legitimate resources available for those who have been seriously hurt after being in a relationship with someone who suffers from BPD.

Since BPD is a very real mental illness that causes severe trauma to the sufferer, it is very politically incorrect to do or say anything that could be misunderstood as a personal attack on the BPD sufferer.

On my Youtube channel, "The One Thing That Heals BPD and NPD Abuse" I have been often accused of stigmatizing the borderline. While this is not true, I totally understand where these people are coming from.

In order for a partner or ex partner of a borderline to heal from the dysfunction of their relationship, it is imperative that they honestly look at the abusive behavior of their

BPD partner. There is no way to do this without revealing the negative underbelly of the behavior of people who suffer from BPD.

I do not identify the behavior of a mentally ill person as being evil. They are human beings who deserve love and respect. If they can become willing to get help, many people with BPD can and do recover and learn how to have healthy, loving relationships. Just like alcoholics are not evil for having an addiction to alcohol, people with BPD are not evil for having a mental illness.

But just as in the case of an untreated alcoholic, while their condition does not define their essence, their behavior can be extremely destructive to other people and those people deserve to have the safety to acknowledge what they survived. And if they are not able to allow themselves to become honest about what they have endured, they will not be able to heal from the trauma.

So, I will be simply sharing with the reader the harsh reality of the nature of BPD in romantic relationships. Because in order to heal, I needed to be honest about what I endured. And I have found that others who have been in my position also benefit from an honest recounting of their experience without being branded as a stigmatizer or a victim blamer.

That is why this book is not meant for people who suffer from BPD, unless perhaps, they have had decades of successful therapy and have a thick skin and are able to hear what it feels like for the non-disordered partner to be in a romantic relationship with a BPD sufferer who is not in a state of recovery.

Because the non-disordered partner has already been trained to minimize and excuse the extremely abusive behavior of the borderline as a result of the codependent dynamic of such a relationship, it is unfortunately necessary for someone to point out the obvious, but unsavory truth: People with BPD can be extremely cruel and abusive.

It is not my desire to stigmatize borderline personality disorder. In fact, I have a deep empathy for the borderline. After decades of therapy I, myself have come to the conclusion that both my mother and brother and perhaps my grandmother suffered from BPD.

While there is no firm consensus on what definitively causes BPD, it is well known that the vast majority of BPD sufferers have survived unimaginable abuse as infants, toddlers and children.

It is amazing that people who have survived such intense abuse are able to function at all. I am being completely truthful when I say that if I were given the power to cure only one illness on earth, it would without a doubt be borderline personality disorder. The pain they endure on a daily basis is unimaginable.

However, while I have the deepest empathy for BPD sufferers, it does not change the fact that the most explosive expression of BPD abuse occurs within the dynamics of a romantic relationship.

Like many abusive relationships, the borderline may be able to hide their mental illness in most situations. They may be able to go to university, get a good job and be a very successful person in society.

If they are able to stay out of romantic relationships, they are often able to live seemingly normal, healthy lives. But, the inner dynamics of BPD really come alive when they are in a romantic relationships.

The partners and ex partners of people with BPD end up getting lost and forgotten. As the borderline is legitimately someone who has suffered unbelievable abuse, they deserve to be given places to go for help.

But, if the partner of a borderline speaks up about the abuse they suffered, the borderline and our codependent cancel culture have difficulty tolerating sharing the spotlight of being victimized.

So, as someone who has not only endured horrific abuse at the hands of people with BPD, but also having found a cure for the pain of BPD abuse, I am here to share what I have learned.

It is also extremely important to understand that if you have been in a romantic relationship with a person with BPD, your pain will NOT go away just because the relationship has ended.

If relationships with borderlines were like every other relationship, when the relationship ended, time would be able to heal the hurt. However, this never happens with someone who has been in a romantic relationship with a person with BPD.

If you have been hurt by a person with BPD, you have been mentally and psychologically entrained by your BPD partner to continue to re-traumatize yourself even in their absence.

As an unconscious survival mechanism, the BPD sufferer has, in effect, given you their mental illness and it will not go away on its own. While you, technically are not a mentally disordered person for just dating a borderline, you have been programmed to get stuck in trauma bond "loop" that never gets shut off without doing the one thing that I will reveal to you at the end of this book.

A good, but unpleasant analogy is that if you have been in a romantic relationship with a borderline, you have been infected with a form of BPD yourself and you will be doomed to relive the trauma you have endured for the rest of your life unless you are able to stop the infection and reverse it.

The good news is that if you are not a mentally ill person, you CAN reverse the damage done to you. This is something the borderline cannot do. While the borderline, if they work very hard at it with the right therapy, CAN learn to arrest their symptoms, they can never be fully cured from their mental illness.

But you CAN find a cure to the pain you are feeling. If you have the willingness to do the simple "One Thing" I suggest.

If you have the patience, I suggest that you wait until the end of this book to learn about the one method I used which has completely healed me from the pain of my romantic relationship with a person with BPD.

Until then, let's get brutally honest with what you have endured…

# Your Relationship Is Not What You Think It Is

If you are dating or even married to a person with untreated borderline personality disorder or are a former partner of someone with BPD, regardless of how long you have been with that person, you do not truly know who that person really is.

If you have been deeply touched by someone with untreated BPD, you are operating from a false belief about that person and about the nature of the relationship itself.

In my experience, if you can become conscious of who that person really is, what your relationship to them really is and what you were really seeking from that person, then you will come to a very harsh awakening to the fact that your understanding about the nature of your relationship with your BPD partner is completely inaccurate.

## What You Believe

If you are romantically involved with a person with BPD, you believe that you are with someone with whom you have a very strong mutual emotional bond… You are wrong.

(For convenience sake I will refer to your borderline as 'she' even if your partner is male)

You believe that she loves you but is just so deeply wounded that when she is just about to let your love truly penetrate her heart and heal the wound that blocks her from being loved by you, the fear takes over her mind and she becomes frightened and sabotages the relationship. That's what you *think* is happening… You are wrong.

You believe that if you could just figure out the perfect sequence of events, words or deeds that you could give to her, she would finally get what she truly needs from you.

And if you could just give her what she finally needs and truly wants from you, she would finally, once and for all let your love heal her... And you would be wrong.

And then, you believe that once she sees that you truly are the one who loves her more than anyone else in the universe, once she sees you are safe and will never leave her or hurt her, THEN she will finally turn around, stop running away from you and give you the love she desperately wants to give you.

You would both finally get the deep, intimate, nurturing love that you both so desperately want and need from each other. That's what she's told you and that's what you believe. And, again... You are wrong.

You believe that even though she is like a scared rabbit, she is, at her core, a rational person who truly loves you, knows what she is doing and that she ultimately has control over her actions even if she doesn't realize that she has this control.

If you could just help her see that she does have control over her actions and doesn't need to act like a scared rabbit, she would gladly change her behavior and let herself do what she truly wants most, which is to love you unconditionally. She just needs to know that you believe in her. This is what she wants at her deepest level. This is what you believe… And you are still wrong.

**It's Just A Matter Of Time**

You believe it's just a matter of time before she will love you like she did that first weekend when you first met her. Your love for her is true and you are patient. You know that if you wait it out, she will eventually get tired of rejecting the love she wants more than anything else.

You believe that your continued efforts to weather her rejections are making progress. You believe that every time she rejects you, hurts you and you still refuse to abandon her that it is making an impact on her and little by little, her will to sabotage your love is weakening… And you are still wrong.

You believe that every time she rejects you and you refuse to leave her that her emotional armor gets reduced a little bit more each time and a little more love gets inside her injured soul bringing her one step closer to feeling and surrendering to your healing love.

You believe that your love is piling up inside her heart and eventually the love will overcome the pain she carries. You believe this is what she wants and needs from you even if she doesn't know it yet.

This is a war for her soul and you are slowly winning this war. It's just a matter of time. You can feel it.

You know that eventually your unwavering love will win over her pain. You believe that she remembers each and every loving act you give to her. And you refuse to let her pain defeat your love for her. So, you keep going.

You believe that she secretly remembers each and every patient act of love on your part and over time, as the individual acts of love on your part add up in her memory, she will rationally be won over by the truth and the inevitability your love for her.

The sheer amount of selfless acts of love for her by you will eventually be undeniable to her rational mind and she will be forced to realize that you love her and she is now safe to just let her love out for you, forever.

You are certain that this is a battle to help her regain her rational understanding of love and reject her irrational fear of abandonment. You are appealing to her damaged rational mind of the silliness of her refusal to be loved.

You are certain that this is a rational argument that you will eventually win. Because you have been rational with her this whole time she has been irrational.

She often tells you when she comes back to you after discarding you that she was just sacred and wasn't thinking straight but now she sees her folly and is ready for your love…

But her fear took over again and she went off to Vegas with that guy again. But, it's OK, she's almost ready to accept the truth of your love for you… almost…

And anyone who is rationally correct in their position will always win over an irrational person, you believe. Because truth will always come out and win the day.

You believe If only you could figure out how to get your love into her heart, she would heal. You believe that all your hard work to convince her of your love is about to pay off. You are sure that it is just a matter of time, maybe tomorrow, until she sees once and for all that she is loved and she will stop hurting you when you keep giving your heart to her.

You really believe success is just around the corner. You almost achieved it last week, remember? You saw it in her eyes. You could see her heart melting as your tears of love streamed down your face as you desperately and patiently sought to prove to her once and for all that your love was real and she was eternally safe in your arms.

If it wasn't for that one little remark you unintentionally said or that one little unconscious glance you made that you don't remember making but she caught it anyway, she would have finally seen that you are the one, her one true soulmate.

You almost pulled it off yesterday, remember? She was just about to surrender forever to your infinite healing love. She was about to give herself to you and you alone. You could feel it. You could see it in her eyes, she was about to give you her heart forever and then, suddenly something in her eyes changed and she closed her heart to you… again. You almost had her. So close… Next time for sure. You won't give up on her or your true love.

So, next time, you think, you'll get it right. She will finally stop struggling against the inevitable karmic truth of your spiritual bond with each other. You believe you will figure out exactly how she needs to be talked to, looked at and touched just the right way and, then, finally, it will all be OK. The walls around her heart will finally and permanently come down. All the pain will come to an end.

Next time… For sure… This is what you believe… and you are more wrong than you can possibly imagine.

The sad truth is that the closer you get to her, the farther away from you she runs.

Your Relationship with your borderline is not and never has been at all what you think it is.

# What Happened? Why Did She Change?

"But how did we get here?" You ask yourself? It wasn't like this at all in the beginning. It was more than perfect. What happened?

In the beginning of your relationship, you each felt a strong emotional and spiritual bond that had the power of many lifetimes.

She made you feel as though you were the only person in the universe who could touch her deeply. She had been hurt and misunderstood by all of her other partners before you who most likely abused her and abandoned her (at least that is what she tells you because she talks a lot to you about all of her exes).

Perhaps her partners were psychopathic narcissists who manipulated, tortured and then discarded her. Perhaps her former partners were weak and unable to handle her passion and so she, reluctantly left them.

It may even be possible that you met her while she was in the process of leaving an abusive relationship and when she saw you, she knew intuitively that YOU were the one she had been looking for her whole life. You were her knight in shining armor who had come to rescue her. She told you as much.

And you felt it too. And it was the most fulfilling moment of your life when you knew in your heart that your love had the power to save and fulfill someone else.

The relationship starts out with immediate intense familiarity. Perhaps on your first date, the two of you talked for hours on end, each of you finishing each other's sentences. You had both been wronged and misunderstood by past lovers. Perhaps the evening ended with a passionate love making session that rivaled the passion of Venus herself.

She gave herself to you in ways you didn't think was possible. And she found in you, vulnerability and tenderness you didn't know you had. She SAW you, ALL of you. And it was amazing. She was a goddess of love. And you were her willing slave and she was yours.

When that first date was all over, after being alone with each other for perhaps just one night or one weekend, you both knew the search was over. You had found your life partner, your twin flame, your soulmate, your other half.

Perhaps you planned your wedding during that first weekend. The two of you, now one perfect unit, began to plan your lives together. Your love was going to change the world.

You, until meeting your borderline, had never been truly seen, appreciated and understood by anyone. Your borderline, however, knows you deeply and intimately. She knew you intimately from the first moment she saw you.

She even knows what you are thinking and what you are feeling at any given moment. She reaches deep into your soul and lights up your spiritual center like no one ever has.

For her, the connection is at least as wonderful perhaps more. Being the perfect love goddess that she is, perhaps she loves you even more than you love her, if that's possible. This is slightly unnerving for you, but who cares? She is the perfect woman. You can make mistakes, she will look past them.

Her love is perfect and she has no fear. You can do no wrong, she tells you. She may even tell you that no one could ever truly understand her the way you do which is why she loves you more than any human could.

She tells you that she knows deeply in her heart that YOU are the one who will bring her ultimate satisfaction. You are perfect for her. You can relax, now. The search for love has ended. She will live her life for one goal: to make you happy forever.

As the relationship begins to unfold in the next few days or perhaps weeks, you find that she not only feels the same deep karmic connection with you that you do for her, but that she also tells you that she prefers to be in your company more than anything else.

She may even say that you are the perfect person for her. She may even say that you are her favorite person. You are her chosen person. She never wants to leave your side. She tells you that when she is in your presence, she feels a safety and comfort that she has never felt before.

She says that being in your presence is what gives her peace. So, she will make sure you are happy because if you are happy, your presence will surround her and make her feel happy.

This sounds amazing to you. She is going to take full responsibility for your total happiness because when you are happy, she is happy. What a deal! This is unbelievable! This is perfect. This is too good to be true. But it is true!… Right?

You find that she loves everything about you. Even the flaws in your body that you are a little shy about her seeing. She loves that aspect the most. You're perhaps a few pounds overweight or underweight, but that is what makes you unique. She likes that body type whatever yours is. In fact, she has fantasized about meeting someone just like you a few years older or younger than her, perhaps with a little bit extra belly fat or bony arms whatever your body type is.

And then, magically you showed up looking exactly as she saw her fantasy lover in her dreams with that extra weight or not enough weight with too much hair or not enough hair, whatever it is that you are.

She has always fantasized about YOU! Or were they psychic premonitions because you are her karmic destiny? Whatever it is about you that makes you unique is the exact combination of traits that she was looking for before you arrived.

No one had ALL of the things she was looking for until YOU showed up. You are everything. You are perfect.

Wow, what a deal!

You also find that you can do no wrong with her. She tells you that she wants to be your perfect partner. She asks you what you want her to be. Since she gets her comfort from being in your presence, she wants to make sure that you are thrilled with her all the time.

Do you want her to lose weight? Gain weight? Do you want her to take up your hobbies. What are your sexual fantasies? She will fulfill all of them. In fact, she may get a little hurt if you don't let her fulfill all your secret sexual fantasies with her and her alone. She wants to know what fantasies you've never dared do to a woman. And she wants you to do it with her so that she will have something no other woman has ever shared with you.

Personal boundaries? She has none. Sexual boundaries? She has no need of those either. You are perfect. You would never harm her. She will surrender to your desires no matter how depraved because they're yours and you are her perfect partner.

Just tell her what she needs to do to be your perfect fantasy girlfriend. No, seriously… TELL her. Tell her now, because if you're not willing to be vulnerable with her with your sexual fantasies, right here and now, then maybe you don't really love and trust her enough…

"I'm giving all of myself to you here." She says, "And you are too scared to just give me that one little thing that I'm asking from you?

Why? Do you have another girlfriend who does that for you? I can't believe you would cheat on me already? I thought you were different! I trusted you!"

(Insert record scratch noise here)

Whoops! Where did that come from? No worries. A slight slip of the tongue from her. When you look slightly confused and the awkward silence brings her momentarily back to reality, she backs off and says she's just kidding and says she needs to go to the bathroom and be right back…

But she stays in the bathroom for 30 minutes with the water running.

But then, she comes back out again and everything goes back to perfect fantasy state like before… even if it feels a little tense in the house from that moment on…

But, that was kind of weird. Wasn't it? Where did that come from? Oh, well, she says she's OK now so, let's just forget that she said that and let things go back to being perfect again. Just a little new relationship jitters or something, you guess.

But, unfortunately that first little glitch in her perfect understanding of you never really gets put back in the bottle. She never really seems to recover from that slight against her that you don't remember making.

Your perfect weekend is coming to an end and the last half of the last day is taken up with a long conversation about how you aren't dating anyone else and that you really DO want to try new sexual practices with her and that you weren't disgusted by her desires and that you really DO still love her and you honestly, you swear, did NOT look at her funny when she talked about her secret desires....

You just want things to go back to the way they were yesterday. What happened to that woman? What did you do wrong? Is there something you can say or do to get her to trust you again?

You feel guilty, but you're not quite sure what you did wrong. All you know now is that you feel a deep hole borrowing its way into your gut.

She comes out of the bathroom after being on the phone with someone that she won't say who it was. She has made herself up again and looks amazing. She tells you that she suddenly needs to get back home. Something unexpected has come up. You offer to give her a ride but she refuses and says she already called an Uber.

You start to apologize for whatever you did to hurt her. She tells you it's not a problem. Don't worry. She'll call you tomorrow or the next day but she just doesn't have time to talk about it right now.

She disappears out the front door without a hug or kiss goodbye and in the silence after the Uber drives away with her in it, you feel an intense anxiety growing inside your gut.

And before you know it, an hour has gone by and you're still staring at the door as if your hard drive has stopped spinning in your head and the message "file not found" is displayed prominently on your forehead.

And you ask yourself, "What the hell just happened?"

You think perhaps your perfect love relationship is over as soon as it began. You wonder how you will recover from this. But, sadly for you, your hell has just begun. And the worst part is, you will never figure out what is really going on with her... Never.

However, you are on a mission now. To figure out once and for all what went wrong, how you can fix it and how you can get that perfect fantasy girl back.

You will devote every waking moment to understanding her. You will learn exactly what her tragic wound is and how you can fix it. She is your true soulmate. You have to fix this.

But, let me just cut to the sad ending of this never ending tragedy. You will NEVER understand who she is and whatever you think you know about her and her connection to you is completely wrong.

In this book, I will show you exactly what REALLY is going on with her and her connection to you. I will show you why you can't forget her no matter how hard you try and I will show you the ONE thing you can do to completely heal from the unbelievable pain this relationship has given to you.

So, if you are reading this book, it is likely that you have been in this rollercoaster with your borderline for a long time and you believe that all of your research into BPD has given you significant insight into your relationship.

But, I am here to tell you, as someone who has completely healed myself of the trauma of a BPD relationship, that no matter how much research you have done into this tragic mental illness and no matter how much work you have done on yourself, you still have no clue who she is, what her connection to you is and what is eventually coming for you if you don't achieve real healing.

That is what this book will do for you, if you read it and follow my suggestions. But, the likelihood of you simply following my suggestions and achieving the complete healing I achieved is slim. Because it is likely that you will refuse to following my suggestions.

Not because the suggestions I give aren't simple. They are extremely simple. It is because you still don't know what is really going on. If you have been bitten by the BPD bug, you have been infected with a false belief that is very persistent.

This false belief that you understand what is going on with her and the false belief that you understand what you really want from her, will do everything in its power to prevent you from following the simple suggestions I will give to you in this book.

Perhaps I am wrong. Perhaps you DO have the willingness to follow the simple instructions I will give you. Many have followed my advice and completely healed from the trauma they experienced from loving a borderline.

But, sadly, many others refuse to follow my simple instructions because they can't let go of the persistent belief that they know why their borderline does what she does and the persistent belief that they understand themselves and why they still chase after her or (if she has completely and permanently discarded them) why they can't stop thinking about their long lost BPD ex, even decades later.

But I will save my instructions until the end. For now, let's look at what is really going on underneath that seductive exterior of your BPD. Let me show you why you have no idea what is really going on with her. Let me show you why your relationship with her is not what you think.

# Your Borderline Is Not Rational

So, the first false belief we need to erase from your mind is that your borderline is a rationally thinking person. Your strategy to get understanding of your borderline stems from the delusion that your borderline is rational and you can appeal to that rationality.

You don't realize that your base assumption about her is that she thinks and feels like you do. She doesn't. But, you unconsciously think that if you can appeal to her rationality, she will be able to hear you and snap out of her irrational thinking and behavior.

You don't consciously realize that you are acting from this delusion. That's not your fault. Because most people are rational. Appealing to people's innate rationality works most of the time. So, you keep trying this same strategy of appealing to her rationality over and over again. But it's not working. That's because she is not rational.

You have been trying to persuade her with rational arguments about your motives and her actions. She cannot be persuaded with rationality. Because her reality is completely different than yours.

She may present herself as a rational person. Especially in the beginning of your relationship or when it comes to anything other than her feelings for you or her destructive actions towards you, she may present herself as extremely self aware and a rational thinker. Until she's not. And then you find yourself dealing with a completely different irrational person who can't understand anything you're saying to her.

You try to keep trying to steer your conversations with her back to that rational person you know is inside of her. And sometimes it seems to work. Sometimes she admits that she is acting out of fear and is OK now. But that never lasts for very long and this irrational person always emerges again, suddenly, out of nowhere at the most inconvenient times just as you are about to get her to realize that you truly love her and then she destroys everything… again.

One of the things rational people do is remember what they have said, done and committed to. You are a rational person which is why it is so confusing and hurtful to you when your borderline either doesn't remember what she said, did or promised and also doesn't accurately remember what you said, did and promise d.

The persistent confusion that you have about your relationship is partly because you unconsciously just assume that the person you are in love with is rational and has a functioning memory of events. She doesn't.

So, your strategy of overcoming her pain with consistent rational, predictable arguments and behavior is a complete waste of time. She remembers none of it.

So, since I haven't said the obvious yet, let's remind ourselves of the elephant in the room. Borderline Personality Disorder is a very serious mental illness.

What is your reaction when you hear me say that your girlfriend or wife is mentally ill? What is mental illness? What is different about someone who has a mental illness and someone who just has serious emotional issues?

Someone with serious emotional issues and is perhaps neurotic is able to be persuaded with rational arguments that bring them back into a comfortable relationship to objective reality.

The best way to address this is to look at these two terms: Psychosis and Neurosis. What is the difference between the two states of being psychotic vs being neurotic?

Psychotic means that someone is not having a coherent relationship with objective reality. They are "crazy." Neurotic means that someone IS having a coherent relationship with objective reality but they don't like objective reality. They're thinking is "crazy" but they can be rationalized with.

For the psychotic person, they have a false understanding of reality. They aren't in conflict with realty. They are in a different reality than the rest of us. Their reality is not based on objective truth, it is based on their internal, narcissistic fantasies. A psychotic person does not know the difference between their fantasies and objective reality.

A neurotic person DOES know the difference between their fantasies and reality and therefore can be talked to rationally. The psychotic person cannot be rationalized with because they cannot be grounded into objective truth because their internal reality keeps shifting based on their internal, narcissistic fantasies.

The Neurotic person is still in the same reality as the rest of us but really wishes things were different. The neurotic person has a lot of anxiety about the reality they perceive and they are struggling with accepting objective reality.

Whereas, the psychotic person is not struggling with objective reality, they have left our understanding reality or, perhaps never shared our understanding of reality. You cannot lead them into objective reality because our objective reality does not exist for them.

Let me remind you of the obvious: You are in love with someone who suffers from a mental illness. They are, at least at times, psychotic. You cannot ground them in objective reality with your rational arguments, because objective reality does not fully exist for them.

This is not a condemnation. This is just a fact. They are mentally ill. Part of your neurosis is the persistent belief that the person you are in love with is neurotic, not psychotic.

If you can accept that your borderline girlfriend is, in fact, in the grips of a mental illness that prevents her from understanding her behavior in a rational way, you will be one step closer to releasing your neurotic desire to try and rationalize with her and get her to accept your love and to love you back.

In order for her to love you the way you want, she would have to be rational. Because she has BPD, by definition, she is incapable of interacting with you in a rational way.

Borderlines aren't struggling with their perception of reality, they are struggling against YOUR perception of reality.

The neurotic person knows that they are in conflict with objective reality and struggles to regain a firm connection to the truth.

A psychotic person struggles not with themselves but with YOU. From their perspective, YOU are the crazy person who is not seeing the truth.

When you have two people who have differing definitions of reality, it makes it difficult for those people to carry on a rational conversation about events they both lived through.

Your borderline is not rational, because she has a mental illness that prevents her from knowing the difference between her inner fantasies and objective reality.

In short, your entire delusion that there is a rational strategy to heal your relationship is coming from your inability or unwillingness to accept the fact that the person you are in love with suffers from a form of psychosis called borderline personality disorder.

If you can accept this, you will be on your way to being able to take the simple steps to heal yourself from the pain you are in.

But first, it may help to understand some of what is really going on in her mind about you and your relationship.

# Your Borderline Doesn't Know You Exist

If you have done any research into borderline personality disorder, you already know of something called "object constancy." And, if you have researched this subject, you already know that your borderline girlfriend suffers from a **lack** of object constancy. And it is a very serious symptom of mental illness.

If someone has healthy functioning object constancy, it means that they remember that you still exist when you leave the room, go to the store for some milk or leave the house to go to work.

For a healthy person, you have been permanently fixed into their mind and they can continue to interact with the memory of you even when you have gone out of town for a week. They will still know you exist and when you return, they can pick up where they left off with you as though you never left. You exist in their mind whether you are physically there with them or not. And they remember you, basically, as you actually are, not as they want you to be.

This is not the case with your borderline girlfriend. She does not remember you, nor does she have an accurate memory of you, even if she was with you just an hour ago.

If someone has a lack of object constancy, it means that when you turn the corner, you literally stop existing for them. They do not have the ability to retain the memory of you. You stop existing the moment you leave their sight.

If you leave the room, she will have to immediately replace you, either in her mind or in physical reality with another caretaker who can be there for her.

That's why she can leave you after spending a romantic weekend getaway and within hours be with another man as though your weekend getaway never happened. Because in her mind, she already forgot about it.

Would you like to know why she so easily went from you to someone else? It wasn't because when she was with you that she didn't love you in that moment. It wasn't because she's an evil person who was planning on cheating on you the whole time.

It is because the moment you kissed her goodbye and left the room, you instantly disappeared from the universe and she needed to replace you with someone else.

She retained no memory of you, your love or anything that transpired between you. This is called mental illness. It is not normal and it is not rational.

If you are someone who does not suffer from a mental illness, then you simply take for granted that when you leave the room, your girlfriend will remember that you exist and more importantly, she will remember that you just pledged your undying love to her and gave her a diamond ring to prove your love.

But, since you don't suffer from a mental illness, you don't realize that the moment you leave the apartment after giving her a diamond ring, that you literally stopped existing in her reality. That diamond ring on her finger does absolutely nothing to alleviate her intense feeling of abandonment. Because in her mind, now, you never existed.

Does it make sense now why your borderline wants to be with you all the time when she's feeling in love with you and you are together? It's not because you are special to her. It's because you are there for her right now and she knows that you will stop existing for her the moment that you leave her sight.

For her, when you leave the room, you have stopped existing and that is the same as if you have abandoned her forever. She can't tolerate that thought, so she tries to keep the perfect fantasy going in her head of being loved and in order to do that, she needs to keep you in her sight or she will be alone again. And being alone for a borderline is intensely painful.

I learned this firsthand with my borderline ex girlfriend whom we will call "Candy." Very early in our relationship Candy was spending the weekend with me at my house. We had been planning our new life together and she suddenly said. "Let's video tape this discussion so that we will remember it."

That sounded a little strange to me, but I said, "Sure, why not?" She must have sensed my slight confusion and said, "No, really this is a very powerful spiritual act. We should videotape our plans for our perfect life."

I went and got my laptop and when I sat back down and positioned the laptop to record, she said, "I sometimes forget things and this will help me remember what you are promising to me. It is a really cool spiritual thing to do."

Because I was still in the whirlwind of infatuation, I chose not to pay attention to the fact that she just admitted to me that even though we were planning our future life together that she would probably forget what she was promising to do for me. It didn't dawn on me that she was saying that she would probably forget that we were planning on getting married and spending our lives together.

But, looking back on it, it is clear to me that in that moment, she was really excited about spending her life with me and she knew that once she went to sleep, she would forget about what she said and what I said.

And as it turned out, even though I did videotape our promises to each other, the very next day, when she woke up, she had forgotten what we both said. And the videotape meant nothing to her.

She knew that she had a lack of object constancy, even if she was not familiar with the term, she knew that she would forget about how intensely she loved me and how much she wanted to make a life with me.

Sadly, for me, because I was not familiar with borderline personality disorder, I did not know to take serious note of the fact that she knew she might forget everything she said and felt. And sure enough, the next day, she discarded me as though I never existed.

I wish that were the end of the story, but after a couple weeks, she came back and told me some excuse about being scared and I believed her and my rollercoaster relationship began again. But I digress…

This happens because someone with borderline personality disorder has not matured beyond the mind of an infant in this regard.

I am not exaggerating here. This mental illness is very serious. People with BPD, especially in regard to romance literally have the mind of an infant. You are in love with someone who has the romantic capacity of an infant in the body of a fully grown adult.

We can understand that an infant is not able to hold on to their memory of you when you leave. For an infant, if you leave, you stop existing. We accept this about babies.

But, we are not trained to assume that a full grown adult cannot conceptualize your existence if you get in the car and go to the store for an hour.

Your borderline girlfriend's mind, when it comes to your existence cannot hold on to the idea that you exist if she cannot see, touch and hear you.

So, what is the result? When you leave the room, you stop existing. When you come back into the room, you are different person to her. If, in her mind, while you were gone, she imagined that you cheated on her with another woman, that is exactly what happened. She cannot tell the difference between the objective you and the you that exists in her mind. If in her mind, you cheated on her, that is who you have become; a narcissistic cheater and abuser of women.

The bottom line is that when you are with your borderline, you think she sees you as an independent person. She doesn't. She sees you as a physical manifestation of the fantasy that exists in her mind. If you are not physically there to help guide that fantasy, her mind will create another reality about who and what you are.

The bottom line is that you do not, nor have you ever truly existed for her. You are nothing more than a physical body that she can project onto whatever is in her mind at that time.

If she wants to see you as perfect, that is what you are. If what she wants to see is that you are a horrible, evil abuser, that is what you are to her no matter what you say or do, or no matter what just happened just a few seconds ago.

One of the most helpful things I read while I was in horrible emotional pain from the most recent discard of my borderline girlfriend was from an article about BPD that went something like this:

**"You must realize that the borderline does not truly see you. What they see is a fuzzy outline of a human being that they can project onto whatever they need at the time. You don't truly exist as an independent person in the mind of a borderline."**

So, if you can understand that you do not, nor have you **ever** existed in the mind of your borderline girlfriend or wife, then you are one step closer to being able to heal from this pain.

This is why even if you have been with your borderline girlfriend or wife for decades, they can discard you like a used candy bar wrapper in a heartbeat and never look back.

You think that because you have been with your BPD girlfriend or wife for years that all of that history and experience carries some weight with them. It doesn't.

You think that they remember all of the time you have spent together. They don't. You think that the fact that you have children with them carries weight with them. It doesn't.

Like an infant, they have no real memories of anything that isn't happening in the moment.

When you wake up every day, your existence, your day is just another day in a long string of days that make up your life. You remember who you are and you have an emotional memory and identification with your past, even if you don't like it, you remember it and identify with it.

When a borderline wakes up every morning, conversely, they do not remember what happened the day before. Worse, yet, if they do remember, they do not emotionally identify themselves with anything they said or did or anything that happened to them the day before.

For them, they have woken up to a life that is not theirs. They have to try and figure out who this person is that they are supposed to be and try to pretend like they remember you and everything else in their life. They don't.

For them every day is like waking up with emotional amnesia. They want to remember but they just can't. And they don't remember you, not in any significant emotional way.

If they do have memories of the day before, they have no emotional connection to it.

Their lives are a movie that they are watching. Whatever they did or said the day before is as meaningful to them as the episode of Friends they watched last night. They do not identify with anything they have said or done in the past. And they don't identify with anything they said to you or did with you.

Because they have no object constancy, they can drop you in a heartbeat and never think twice about it because it never really had any deep meaning to them anymore than you would have a deep meaning in the mind of an infant that you held in your arms yesterday. That infant does not remember you. It only knows what it feels right now and you are not there, so you do not, nor have you ever existed for that infant.

Your borderline suffers from a very serious mental illness that curses them to live life exactly like that infant. No matter how much they want you to be real and no matter how much they want to wake up from the continually fading dream they live in, they cannot. They have a mental illness that prevents them from doing so.

The sooner that you can realize that you do not exist in the mind of a borderline, the sooner you can start to heal.

But as long as you try to rationally convince your borderline girlfriend how much you love her and how much she loves you, you are doomed to repeat this hamster wheel of hell.

Are you ready to get off the hamster wheel yet? No? You still have hope it can work? Then let's talk about splitting.

Why does your borderline girlfriend love you more than anything in the universe in one moment and literally within seconds she decides you are the most evil person that ever existed?

This is because your borderline has a mental illness that causes her to "split" at the worst possible times.

# Why Your Borderline Girlfriend "Splits"

So, let's be honest, there are a lot of things that borderlines do that are very hurtful, confusing and destructive. But, that's true with a lot of people. However, we would be able to handle most of those things. But there is one thing that borderlines do that we can't seem to handle. That is when they split on us.

The one thing she does that we can't handle is when she changes in literally a split second from loving you more than anything else in the universe to suddenly, and without warning, hating you more than anything else in the universe.

This is the most confusing, traumatizing and difficult aspect to your borderline girlfriend's behavior. And whatever you think the reason is for her "splitting" on you, you are probably wrong.

"Splitting" is a psychological term that describes what happens when a borderline suddenly changes from one extreme in their feelings for you to the exact opposite. They "split" on you.

Splitting is not a random event, it is actually a very predictable occurrence to anyone on the outside of the relationship who has any experience with being split on by a borderline. I can predict when a borderline will split on someone, if I know the circumstances leading up to the split.

But, when it happens to YOU, when you're the one inside the relationship, it will ALWAYS happen when you least expect it.

In fact, the split will happen most often when you are in that rare moment in your borderline relationship when you are feeling completely secure. You just start to finally relax into feeling like, "This just might work out after all. It's gonna be OK." Then, all of a sudden it is a total nightmare.

Borderlines usually split on their partner right when the partner has become convinced that they have finally, or are just about to finally achieve the deepest intimacy possible in their relationship. And the partner, falsely believes that it is intimacy that will finally fix the borderline. And they couldn't be more wrong.

Even though the borderline keeps telling you that more intimacy is what she needs and if you just knew how to give the right kind of intimacy at the right times, in the right ways, she would be happy and never leave you.

She actually believes this, but both you and she are as wrong as is possible. Intimacy is the very thing that forces the borderline to split on you.

The borderline splits most often when the partner believes they have finally figured out exactly what the borderline wants and needs and is now ready to allow herself to be loved and to love him in return.

"It's over" The partner thinks to himself, "She finally told me what she was *really* afraid of. I finally got through to her that she is safe with me and I would never hurt her. She promised me last night that she would never change on me again, now that she knows that I really do love her. The look in her eyes proved it. She's for real this time. She's going to finally stop hurting me. She promised she would never leave me or cheat on me again. And this time, it's for real. I finally did it. I finally got her to love me forever."

And then, when he is feeling the safest he's ever felt in their relationship in months or even years, she suddenly splits on him and calls him a narcissist abuser who has been planning on poisoning her eggs and making her infertile or some such incredible thing.

The splitting usually occurs when the couple have just experienced a deeply intimate bonding experience.

There was an unbelievably intimate lovemaking session followed by pillow talk that lasted for hours. They fell asleep in each others' arms and then suddenly, at breakfast the next day, when the non-disordered partner was just about to propose marriage, the borderline suddenly snapped and accused her partner of cheating on her with the waitress that smiled at them. And the rollercoaster of hell continues and the partner realizes he's fallen for it again.

But, here's the worst part. Even though he, at this moment, once again, consciously knows that she's mentally Ill and is incapable of loving him. He still can't leave her. By this time, after splitting on him once again, she has blocked his phone, his facebook and email.

She has moved out and slashed his tires. He finds out that she has been sleeping with his asshole, abusive cousin for over 6 months and right after breakfast, she went over to his house and they went off to Vegas together and got married.

If you're reading this and it doesn't sound like the most preposterous comedy you've ever read. That's because you, my friend have experienced this kind of craziness. If you do not laugh out loud, but want to cry instead, it means you have been infected by your borderline. And that infection is incurable, without the one cure I will share with you later in this book.

The situation I just described is absolutely ludicrous. Anyone who has not been in a romantic relationship with a borderline would think that I was exaggerating for comedic effect. But, the example I have just given of what happens when a borderline splits on you, is actually mild compared to the utterly ridiculous lengths some borderlines will go when splitting on their partner.

Someone unfamiliar with this scenario would read this and say, "Well, that would never happen to me. I would see this coming a mile away. I would have left that crazy bitch long before she could do something like that to me."

And I would have said the same thing before my borderline relationship. But having been in similar situations with my borderline ex, I realize that nobody ever consciously chooses to end up in this pathetic position.

The thing about borderlines is that they are so completely different in the beginning. They seem to know exactly what to say and do to get you to drop your guard and give them access to the deepest, most vulnerable parts of yourself. And once they gain access to that part of you and love the part of you that has never been seen and loved before, you don't realize how attached you become to that person.

So, when the person who has the deepest part of your love suddenly splits on you and treats you like you are the most evil being on the planet, as much as you may want to, you can't leave.

Most likely the borderline has left you and told you she never wants to see you again. Even though you know this is the end, you still can't let go.

You can't stop thinking about her. What could I have done differently? What could I have said differently? If I could just figure out whatever the trigger was that pushed that fear button in her, I would never do it again.

She would never be afraid again and then she would never leave me. If only I could figure out what that ONE thing was that I could do or not do that would prevent her from splitting…

Then, you start to research everything you can about borderline personality disorder. Maybe that's why you are reading this book.

You are determined to understand her pain and be the most understanding, loving person in the world for her. You are on a mission. You have been able to turn your miserable pain of loneliness into a spiritual quest for redemption.

Y'know, now that you think about it, you realize that this was the best thing that could have ever happened to you. You realize that by working tirelessly on yourself to be the perfect loving partner for her, that you will evolve spiritually and psychologically like never before. And because of your evolved spiritual nature as the result of this hard work, you will be the only person who can support her through her mental illness.

She will see that you are the only one who truly understands and respects her. She will see after that asshole of a cousin you have who she is sleeping with now turns on her, she will come running back to you and THIS time, you'll know exactly what she needs.

Perhaps, you'll give her this book. If she could just understand that her behavior is a result of a mental illness, she might be able to change her behavior.

But sadly, my friend, none of your hard work will mean anything and none of your hopeful fantasies for a better future will ever arise between you and your borderline.

And the reason is because you do not understand what is happening when she splits on you. If you can truly absorb the truth of what is happening inside the mind of your borderline when she splits on you, you will be one step closer to doing the ONE thing that can heal you from all this pain.

So, what is REALLY going on when she splits on you? Bear in mind what we talked about in the previous chapter where you learned that your borderline does not really see you.

This is important. Because your belief that your ability to help her when she splits on you is based on your false belief that she sees you and your true intentions. She doesn't. She never has.

In order for her to avoid splitting on you, she has to have the ability to see you and remember who you really are. She has to be able to say to herself, "I'm just really scared of how intimate this feels. I just need to focus on the man who is in front of me and not on the fear based fantasy that my mind has created in order to scare me."

But in order for her to do that, she has to actually have a true picture of you in her mind that doesn't disappear every 30 seconds.

Because she doesn't see you and because she doesn't remember what you just said 10 minutes ago, she doesn't have the ability to anchor herself in a real understanding of you and talk herself out of her fear.

So, what is really happening when she splits?

Like me, (and probably your borderline thinks this too), you might think that what is happening is that when the love becomes too real, it triggers her fear of abandonment which then triggers a self-defense response in an attempt to avoid being hurt.

NOPE. Sounds good on paper, but that is not what is REALLY going on. If you can handle what is REALLY going on with her and accept it, you may be able to separate from her emotionally and do what is necessary to heal yourself.

OK, strap yourself in. Here is what she is REALLY doing when she splits on you.

She is NOT running away from true love because it frightens her. She may also think that is what she is doing. But what she is really doing is going to BLOW your mind. You ready for it? Here it comes…

When she splits on you, she is actually shifting into another personality that will psychopathically punish you for loving her.

That's right she isn't just running away, she is punishing you, not for doing something bad, but for unconditionally loving her exactly as she asked you to do.

She is punishing you for giving her the very thing she says she wants. And she will always punish you every time that you successfully make her feel loved.

The idea that your love is slowly melting her cold heart is false. Your continued love for her is awakening and strengthening a monster inside of her who only grows stronger and stronger every time she gets a little bit closer to you. Your love cannot ever reach her. EVER.

Have you noticed that each time she splits on you, she gets meaner and meaner? Have you noticed that the time between splits is getting shorter and shorter? Have you noticed that when she comes back to you after each split that she feels a little colder and more removed? Have you noticed that she has NEVER turned back into that first perfect love partner that she was in the very beginning?

Here's what is really happening with her… In order to understand this, you have to understand how she became a borderline to begin with.

According to most psychologists, borderlines are created in infancy.

Did you know that lack of intimate contact with an infant is more deadly to them than lack of food and shelter?

There have been numerous experiments over hundreds of years that have proven that even if you feed, clothe and take care of the physical needs of an infant, if that infant does not get continuous intimate interaction with an adult, that infant will die… every time.

Literally an infant will die from lack of love long before she dies from lack of food or shelter.

Your girlfriend, when she was an infant, was not neglected enough to kill her. She got just enough attention to avoid dying from lack of love, but the trauma of being neglected in her crib broke the part of her mind that gives most people the ability to have successful loving relationships.

It is not uncommon for borderline adults to have been left alone as infants for hours or days at a time. And this extreme neglect is what destroys their mind.

The trauma her brain and nervous system endured is not something that can ever be cured. It is impossible for your love to heal her… ever.

Here's the worst part. In her mind, she is still that neglected infant desperately seeking the love and nurturing from her parents.

Now, in a healthy mind, the person matures beyond puberty and begins to create a separate identity from their parents. This process is called "individuation" and it is the ultimate goal of all psychotherapy and spiritual practice.

But, for the borderline, she can never evolve beyond the infantile state of completely identifying with the parent. She is her mother and her mother is an abusive psychopath.

So, in the beginning, the reason why you seem so perfect to her is because in the beginning of the relationship, she is successfully transferring her attachment to her mother onto you. When she looks at you in those first days of the relationship, she doesn't see you, she sees her mother.

This works really well for the borderline in the beginning which is why you can do no wrong in her eyes at first. She looks at you and sees her mother finally loving her and giving her the attention she so desperately needs.

This is also why, in the beginning, she doesn't want to be away from you even for a moment. That's because in her mind, she is a needy infant and you are her mother and being apart from her mother when she was an infant was extremely traumatic for her. That's why she freaks out when you leave the room.

If this dynamic never changed in her mind, perhaps she would never split on you.

But something even more insidious starts to happen in her mind which will ultimately completely destroy the relationship.

In her mind, she becomes aware that you are not her mother and she realizes (on an unconscious level) that if she transfers her infantile love onto you, she will be rejecting her own psychopathic mother existing inside her mind. For an infant, being connected to the mother is the most important tool for her survival.

So, in an attempt to protect her from someone who is threatening to take away her mother from her (you), she then creates a a psychopathic protector personality who seeks to destroy anyone that threatens to take away her mother from her.

So, when your borderline splits on you, it is not the needy little infant who truly does appreciate your love and attention, it is a second personality hidden deep in the borderline's unconscious that is bursting forth on the scene to destroy any person that threatens to take away the infant from her mother.

Unconsciously, this hidden psychopath is always continuously attacking, criticizing and belittling the vulnerable, loving infant part of her mind. She is continuously punishing herself for not being good enough to have deserved her mother's love.

On an unconscious level, the borderline believes that it is her duty to be alone and miserable because in a twisted way, her mind has convinced her that if she punishes herself harshly enough, that her mother will finally love her and end her misery.

You see, the ONLY person in the world who has permission to love her is her mother. And if her mother was unavailable, narcissistic, or most likely, a borderline herself, her mother will never, ever love her.

This is the script in her head. This is the script that has been programmed into the neurons of her brain and nervous system since she was an infant. There is no amount of psychotherapy that can ever completely reverse this dynamic.

There is no human on the planet that can ever give her the love she needs.

So, because she has created this inner psychopath to simultaneously prevent her from betraying her internalized mother and protect her from anyone who threatens to replace her mother, your relationship with her was doomed before it ever started.

How this dynamic will play out in your relationship with your borderline is that in the beginning, you actually DO replace her mother and she feels completely loved for the first time in her life. (Btw, she feels this for every single romantic partner she ever had so don't think it has anything to do with how amazing you are.)

But as soon as she starts to allow herself to feel safe in your arms and finally starts to love you back, the inner psychopath, who has been watching the two of you the whole time, suddenly and violently emerges from the depths of her unconscious to savagely beat back ANY intruder who threatens to take away the infant from her abusive internalized mother.

Because she is programmed to believe that her unworthiness for love is the only hope to eventually get mom to love her, if you succeed in making her feel loved, you are sabotaging her connection to her mother and the inner psychopath will have to immediately eliminate you from her life.

This whole time you have been, understandably thinking that if you are patient and keep showing her that you love her, she will eventually realize that you are a safe person to love.

But what is really happening, is that every time you survive her splitting and allow her to come back into your life, you become a more dangerous threat to her infantile dream of getting her abusive mother to finally love her.

What this means is that every splitting action your borderline makes against you will get worse and worse until there is a final discard where she will never return for you again.

Instead of being able to convince your borderline girlfriend that you are the only one who truly loves her, you will be stimulating an ever increasing psychopathic defense response to your love.

As a result of my Youtube channel, I have interacted with hundreds of people just like you, who have confirmed that no matter how many decades you stay with a borderline, unless they have gotten professional help and stuck with counseling for at least 10 years, the borderline will eventually split on you, one last time. And that last split will be the most abusive, destructive experience of your life.

It is what I call the "Final Discard." If you are in any kind of contact with your borderline after having been romantic with her, you can be assured that one day, perhaps decades from now, your borderline will split on you in the worst possible way and will destroy the relationship to such a degree that it can never be repaired.

And, if you last long enough to experience a final discard, you will be reduced to a shadow of your former self. You will limp along for the rest of your life infected with a form of BPD yourself.

I've seen it over and over again. This is what is waiting for you if you stay with your borderline. UNLESS, you do the one thing that can heal you.

# Is Your Borderline Girlfriend Evil?

In my experience with my youtube channel, there are basically only two reactions people have to their borderline's behavior.

1) She is traumatized and needs me because nobody else understands or supports her.

2) She is an evil genius and has been planning my demise this whole time.

In this chapter, I will show you why both of those reactions are ineffective and inaccurate. I will especially show you why, if you think your borderline is evil, that you still love her and want her back.

Let's start with reaction #1:

If you relate to reaction number 1, that your borderline is just a misunderstood, traumatized victim and that you are the only person that she can trust to talk to about her problems, then you are still in the early denial phase of the relationship. (Just to be clear, the denial phase can last for decades in some cases.)

The denial phase is pretty straight forward. You are in denial that your relationship is doomed. You are in denial about the fact that your borderline, does not love you, is not making progress and is not going to eventually grow out of her continued splitting on you. In essence, you still have hope that the relationship will ultimately work if you just hang in there long enough.

The denial phase can also include the dreaded "friend zone." I cannot tell you how many people on my channel are stuck in the friend zone. I was in the friend zone for a short bit myself. The friend zone guys are even in denial that they still want a romantic relationship.

They have deluded themselves into believing they are some kind of superhero who no longer has any selfish need for love from anybody. They just want to help their borderline friend.

The friend zone often times includes intermittent bouts of fuck buddy episodes.

The borderline has been very clear that she is no longer interested in a committed romantic relationship with you, but in between other abusive partners, she will retreat back into the arms of you, the friend/fuck buddy when it is convenient for her.

The friend zone does not guarantee sex for you at any time. In fact, your borderline may seek you out only for money or consolation if her current narcissistic boyfriend is being an asshole, so you never allow yourself to fully surrender to the relationship idea again (or so you tell yourself).

She may even tell you that even though she needs a place to stay for the weekend that she is not going to have sex with you.

But, you secretly know that in the middle of the night she will crawl into bed with you and have sex with you. And then she may even wake up the next day and deny that you had sex with her last night.

But you do really love it when she decides that she wants to use you just for sex. Even if it gives you some feeling of intimacy, just for a day or so.

Of course, even though you know you're just a friend to her and nothing more, when the sex ends and she puts her makeup back on for your asshole cousin that she's going home to right now and suddenly leaves you again while you are still naked in bed after accusing you of abusing her in some strange way you don't quite understand…,

Once again that familiar black hole of desperation takes over one more time. She slams the door behind her. You can still smell her on the sheets and you can't believe the pain that suddenly engulfs you as you hear the Uber car drive away with her in it as you stare at the door while your hard drive in your brain starts to spin out of control.

Now, because you are still in denial and, in truth, you are still hoping she will remember how you are the one who truly loves her, you hope during one of these fuck buddy episodes, she will decide to finally come back to you and marry you.

As long as there is still any kind of connection, you still have hope that one day it will all work out… And, it never does.

But, even though, she never does come back to you like that first time, that first wonderful weekend you spent together… She hints at it sometimes and you start to get hope, but then, you say the wrong thing and she storms out of your house and goes back to your asshole cousin in Vegas with whom she has a couple of fucked up kids.

And then you remind yourself that you are just her friend and you just want to help her because nobody else listens to her. And your anxiety increases and your hell of loneliness continues.

This is one manifestation of reaction #1 Reaction #1 will last for as long as you think there is any hope whatsoever and/or if you have any contact with your borderline even if it is very sporadic.

But, eventually reaction #1, specifically, the delusion that you are just friends and that you really want nothing selfishly from her, will disappear and will suddenly and ferociously transform into reaction #2 where you convince yourself that she was really just an evil genius who was planning your demise this whole time.

Unless you do the one thing that can cure you, you will inevitably shift to reaction #2 where you wake up one day and reluctantly come to the inescapable conclusion that she really is gone forever and is never coming back.

You see that there is absolutely no hope of her ever returning to you and then, you will shift into a NEW false belief that she is an evil narcissist who was planning to do this to you the whole time.

You rightly conclude that she never truly loved you, but you mistakenly believe that she was planning on hurting you the whole time you were together.

You believe that she planned your pain that you are feeling right now from the moment she first saw you.

You realize that she never meant anything she said, but only said those things to get you to love her so that she could use you, destroy you and throw you away and then laugh about it behind your back.

Perhaps you have given her money or gifts or cars that she is still using while she fucks your asshole cousin and they both laugh at your gullibility while they drink champagne that you gave to her last year.

You don't know if this is going on or not, which also drives you crazy, but you are pretty sure that is what is going on inside your asshole cousin's trailer every night.

You don't realize this, but your need to believe that she is an evil genius who planned your demise is actually a sign that you STILL love her and want her back.

You may not have any hope that she will come back, but that is the reason you are so angry. It is because she still owns you and you cannot accept the idea that she has completely rejected you.

And this makes you furious. Perhaps only on an unconscious level. If your rage is unconscious, you just go numb and can't feel anything.

If you are not numb with unconscious rage, you indignantly deny this ridiculous allegation of mine that you still want her back.

You froth at the mouth on internet forums and youtube comment sections about how evil and narcissistic your borderline was. You protest vehemently against any idea that you would take her back if she hoovered you again.

You actually believe that you would never be with her again no matter how much she begged for you to let her come back. In fact, you fantasize about how you would torture her with your refusal.

You imagine that she probably still realizes deep in her heart that you were the only one who truly loved her and you relish the thought that you would tell her repeatedly how horrible she was to you and that there is nothing she could ever do to make you trust her again.

This would, of course devastate her, you fantasize, but you don't care. She deserves it!

In fact, you rehearse what you would say to her to torture her as she begged you for forgiveness.

You imagine she is kneeling before you begging you for mercy. You even start to fantasize about how you might just use her for sex and throw her away just like she did to you.

You honestly believe this story you tell yourself that you could never take her back. You believe the rage and anger you feel protects you from her if she ever decided to come back.

But the truth is, if she did come back to you, you would take her back in a heartbeat. Perhaps you would complain a little about how much she hurt you and if she told you anything that made you feel she was even the slightest bit sorry for her actions, you would then realize once again, that she is your soulmate and even though you're still a little hurt, you would get right back to your earlier project of proving your love to her and finally getting her to go back to that person that you first met all those years ago.

The message of this chapter is, If you hold any resentment toward her whatsoever, it means you still want her back.

The opposite of love is not hate or anger. The opposite of love is apathy. If you are not truly indifferent, then you still love her.

There is a way to be completely free of your pain, hopelessness, anger and sadness. But, if I am honest, even though it is very simple to do, statistically, you won't do what it takes to be free. Perhaps, I am wrong about you. If you follow my suggestions, them I am wrong and you can heal.

If you refuse to follow my suggestions, then I was right about you and you still are addicted to being abused. You will decide for yourself as I am not there with you to see whether or not you do the simple thing that can heal you.

In the next chapter, we will explore how even though you consciously are aware that she suffers from BPD, you still don't understand that she has a mental illness.

# Why You Can't Accept Your Borderline Is Mentally Ill

As I said earlier, you may consciously understand that she has borderline personality disorder, but if you are still holding on to any hope for a relationship with your borderline girlfriend or if you are full of rage believing your borderline ex is an evil narcissist, then you do not understand that your borderline is mentally ill.

Let me stress to you again, the obvious fact that you cannot or you refuse to see: Borderline Personality Disorder is a very serious mental illness that has no cure.

(read that last paragraph one more time)

BPD is most explosively expressed in romantic relationships. What you are asking this person to do for you is impossible.

It is very tragic that the very thing the borderline wants from you most of all is the very thing that will trigger a psychopathic, psychotic response toward you.

This will never change. If you have any hope that it can change, then you are in neurotic state yourself.

Remember the difference between psychosis and neurosis? Neurosis is the state of mind where you consciously know what objective reality is but your struggle against it.

You know it's true but you don't like it.

So, when you get together with your borderline, your neurosis and her psychosis fits together like a drum. But that connection you share is doomed because your neurosis is seeking to reunite with objective reality and her psychosis is seeking to pull you into her psychotic fantasies.

You can't live in her world and she can't live in yours. That is a fact. There is nothing that can be done to fix that.

But what about if my borderline girlfriend gets into therapy? Can we make it work then?

I would be lying if I said that this was impossible. There is a very slight chance that your relationship could work if she got into therapy. And I am taking a huge risk in admitting this to you because it may only serve as a way to enable you to stay in your neurotic delusions.

The reality is that the statistical probability that if you got your borderline into therapy that she would then be able to be a loving partner to you is virtually impossible.

For any borderline reading this, it doesn't mean you can't get counseling and reduce your symptoms and find love. It means that the dynamic of a borderline being sent to therapy by their codependent partner ever resulting in a functioning relationship is extremely unlikely.

Borderlines can and do find recovery in therapy. But, based on my research, it takes at least ten years of intense work to even begin to learn how to manage your BPD symptoms.

So, for the codependent boyfriend who thinks that if he can just get his borderline girlfriend into therapy that then she will return to that perfect fantasy lover that he first met… Sorry, champ. It ain't gonna happen.

Here's what you can expect if you were able to nag your girlfriend into therapy…

She will resent you for it and refuse to take the therapy seriously. But, just for argument's sake, even if she did listen to you and she DID take her therapy seriously, you know what would happen?

In your mind, if she took her therapy seriously, she would become aware of how badly she hurt you and how destructive her behavior is and the awareness of it all would steer her toward becoming that wonderful loving person you first met. But, actually if she took her therapy seriously, the opposite would happen. She would realize that YOU were very bad for her recovery and she would STILL break up with you.

WHY?

Because, she never truly saw you or loved you. You were only someone she transferred and projected onto. She would become aware that projecting and transferring on to other people was damaging to HER. If she gets real with her therapy, she will become aware that the entire relationship with you, both the good times and the bad times were a very destructive way of living for HER.

If you are not in therapy yourself and doing the one thing I suggest, then she will realize that you were also abusing her in your own passive aggressive way and that even wanting her to go to therapy is your selfish way of trying to force into becoming your fantasy girl.

The bottom line is that if your relationship with your borderline girlfriend has any chance of succeeding, then she would have to be celibate for at least 10 years AWAY from all contact with you, before she could even begin to start thinking about being in a romantic relationship with anyone.

So, do you really want to go complete no contact with her and wait 10 years for the possibility of revisiting the possibility of dating you again from scratch as a brand new person?

If you seriously want to be alone for 10 years waiting for her to get better and then expect her to want to be with you, you are kidding yourself.

The other reality is that the only way for your relationship to work is if you get therapy and do the one thing I suggest for the 10 year period while she is working on yourself. And the reality of that scenario is that you, most likely, will realize that you TOO were just transferring and projecting on to HER this whole time.

You will realize that being with an abusive borderline is not what you want. You will realize that there are millions of non-disordered women out there who would love to date you and have no need to split on you or abuse you in any way.

As you begin to heal, you will lose your attachment to your borderline ex and you will look for someone who can love you and see you for who you are. You will start to realize that there are millions of women who will be so grateful for your love and attentiveness and they will never punish you for loving them.

In short, if your borderline girlfriend gets into therapy, she will probably leave you for very healthy reasons. And if you stay with your untreated borderline girlfriend, she will definitely leave you. So, no matter how you look at it, your borderline girlfriend is going to leave you and there is nothing you can do to stop that.

If you truly love your borderline girlfriend the kindest and most loving thing you can do for her is to say,

*"I love you and I want what is best for you. I have come to realize that this relationship is damaging to me and it is in my best interest if I cut off all contact with you. I also realize that what is best for you is to go to therapy for your BPD and if I am still around, I will only make that more difficult for you. So, I am saying goodbye. I hope you seek out therapy. That is your business, though not mine. But, sadly, I must say goodbye to you. I love you and wish you every good thing in life."*

And then after you have sent her this email or text, you immediately go complete no contact with your borderline.

Let me be clear what "going no contact" means. It does not mean that don't initiate contact with her. It doesn't mean that you don't call her but she still has your number, email or facebook contact and you silently wait by the phone for her to call you.

"No contact" means that you make it **impossible** for her to ever contact you, ever again in this lifetime.

(read that last paragraph again)

If you work together, quit and get another job. If you live in the same city, move. If you have kids together, then hire a lawyer and have the lawyer do all the negotiating about visitation.

No contact is absolutely necessary for you to be able to do the one thing that can cure you. If you think my version of no contact is unreasonable or difficult, I didn't say it was easy, I said it was necessary.

Do it or don't do it. But you will find out what happens to your resolve if you don't go no contact.

OK so now that you've given your final goodbye to your borderline girlfriend, now I will finally tell you what I did that **completely cured me from the pain of borderline abuse** in the next chapter.

# The ONE Thing That Heals BPD and NPD Abuse

OK, hopefully you have resisted the temptation to skip to the end and get to the the ONE thing that can heal you without reading the entire book in order. I'm almost sure that you are reading this before having read the entire book. I know you better than you realize.

But, if you are skipping ahead, I will make a feeble attempt to persuade you to stop here now and go back and read this book from the beginning. No? Oh, well, I tried…

So what is the ONE thing that cured me from the pain of borderline abuse? Before I get to that, it is important that you realize that there is absolutely no hope whatsoever for you to have any kind of successful, fulfilling romantic relationship with someone who suffers from a mental illness like BPD. If you are not convinced of that yet, then go back and read this book from the beginning. This only works if you know there is no hope.

Your BPD cannot nor will she ever be able to love you. That is not your fault. She has an incurable mental illness that is most destructive and brings out the most psychopathy when she is in a romantic relationship. If you can't accept that, it is very likely you won't follow my simple suggestions.

And, in my experience, talking with hundreds of people just like you, if you don't follow my simple suggestions, you will never fully heal from the addictive misery that borderlines infect their romantic partners with.

So, let's briefly review what my suggestions are. Even though I have gone into some detail about what is really going on with your borderline girlfriend and even though I have made some pretty strong arguments stating that your relationship is doomed, I have only made one suggestion so far. I have three more suggestions, but only ONE of them is mandatory.

Here are the simple suggestions best done in this precise order.

**Suggestion #1**

I have already given to you the first suggestion which is to **go complete no contact.**

I have suggested that you go "no contact" with your borderline, meaning that you must do absolutely everything you can in order to make it **impossible for your borderline girlfriend to ever contact you ever again for the rest of your life**.

That means doing any or all of the following in order to insure she never successfully contacts you again:

**Block her phone**

**Block her email**

**Change your phone number**

**Block all forms of social media (especially facebook)**

**Move to a new city if necessary**

**If you have kids, *only communicate through a lawyer.***

**If she's a stalker, *get a restraining order against her*.**

Do WHATEVER it takes to make sure she can never contact you again. (I can't over stress this point)

If you are not willing to go complete no contact, it is almost guaranteed you will get back together with her and she will destroy you.

Alright, now let me get to my second suggestion:

Suggestion #2

Go online and type in www.CODA.org look for the next online zoom meeting or an in-person meeting (whichever comes first), raise your hand, get a sponsor and start working the 12 steps (with a sponsor) *immediately*.

What is important is that you work ALL 12 STEPS WITH A SPONSOR. Take note that I did not say go to a bunch of meetings.

Meetings are necessary in the same way that water is necessary to swallow a pill that will save your life. If you just drink the water and not take the pill, you will still die.

If you go to meetings and don't work the steps with a sponsor, you will not heal.

THE WHOLE POINT OF GOING TO MEETINGS IS WORKING THE 12 STEPS.

**Suggestion #3**

The third suggestion is to find a psychologist and start getting professional counseling. It is best if your therapist has experience working with codependents who have suffered narcissistic abuse or PTSD.

**Suggestion #4**

Do some kind of meditation on a daily basis. Any kind of meditation will work. But it works best if it is some kind of meditative discipline like zen meditation, kundalini yoga, mantra meditation, yoga, tai chi, etc… These kinds of traditional meditation disciplines are very good for helping you to rewire the neurons of your brain.

Now, perhaps you are confused. I said that there was only ONE thing that guaranteed a complete cure for borderline abuse, I have just given you four things to do.

You are correct, while it is best for you if you do all four suggestions, there is only ONE thing that is required for you to do if you want to experience the complete cure that I experienced.

If you do the ONE thing that I require for you to experience the healing I have had, then you will eventually start to do the other three things naturally.

BUT if you do the other three things and NOT do the ONE thing, it is very likely that you will never completely cure yourself of the pain of BPD abuse. And you may still end up with another borderline or narcissist.

So, what is the ONE thing out of all those four that I require you to do to heal?

The ONE thing that I am requiring for you to do to completely heal is suggestion #2: *Working the 12 steps with a sponsor and then sponsoring someone else through the twelve steps*

I suggested going to Codependents Anonymous because that is the 12 step program that is most generally relevant to basic codependence. Since you have been infected with the abuse of a borderline, you are by definition a codependent.

I know some of you want to argue with me about that but after hundreds of people just like you who want to argue with me on my YouTube channel about whether or not you are codependent or not, I am just bored with the whole discussion.

Believe me or not, your arguments trying to convince me that you are not a codependent, while they sound rational to you change nothing.

If you have been with a borderline for any length of time, you are by definition a codependent. Whether you like that or not is not my problem.

But, CODA is not the only 12 step group that will work to help you heal from your borderline abuse. ANY 12 step group will work as long as you WORK ALL 12 STEPS WITH A SPONSOR and then become willing to sponsor someone else.

If you have any addictions in your past like alcohol, drugs, sex, gambling, etc, feel free to choose whatever 12 step program you prefer.

The only requirement here is that you work all 12 steps with a sponsor and especially that you focus at least some of your 4th step on your borderline abuser.

The fourth step is crucial. Your pain is superglued to your conscious and unconscious anger toward your abuser.

Even if you are someone who is numb and can't feel your rage toward your borderline abuser, trust me that anger is still there and if you don't work through it, you WILL suffer.

I know some of you already think that you have forgiven your borderline abuser and you have "worked through your anger" etc.,

But, if you are in pain, or you still think about your borderline ex, I guarantee you that you have not truly understood the dynamics of your resentment and you have not worked through it.

I can't over stress this point enough. Until you have worked the fourth step according to the twelve step written materials, you haven't truly uncovered what is driving your pain.

Again, believe me or not, I don't care. Either work the steps or don't. If you really disagree with me, there is one foolproof method to disprove me once and for all. That is to work all 12 steps with a sponsor, then sponsor someone else through all 12 steps.

If you can do that and you still have unresolved pain and/or you still obsess on your borderline ex, then you can come on to my YouTube channel and tell me how wrong I was.

I have given that challenge to everyone who wants to tell me that the 12 steps won't work for whatever reason and not ONE of them has taken me up on that challenge.

However, every single person who HAS followed my suggestions fully have all experienced a massive healing in regard to their borderline relationship pain.

And if you aren't willing to do the work for yourself to find out if it works or not, your arguments are meaningless because you will have no experience to back up your claims.

I have been where you are now. And I am in a completely different mental, emotional and spiritual state now. And I know the difference between the two states. If you haven't done what I have done, you don't know if there even is a difference.

Again, do it or don't do it. It's completely up to you.

I am completely free of anger or pain associated with my borderline ex girlfriend. Can you say the same?

If you're still on the fence and you need more convincing, I invite you to go to my free YouTube channel about this subject entitled

**The ONE Thing That Heals BPD and NPD Abuse**

On that YouTube channel you can watch me over the span of 2.5 years as I worked the 12 steps on my borderline relationship breakup.

If you watch the videos in order, you will see a definite change in my appearance, attitude and message. Besides showing you how fast you can recover from narcissistic abuse, you will hear my deep discussions about the nature of borderline personality disorder, codependence, narcissism in general and most importantly, the ONE thing that heals BPD abuse.

I have no axe to grind. I am not selling any special seminars. I'm not using this book as a means to get life coaching clients to heal from narcissistic abuse.

I am not trying to get you to sign up for anything. I am simply sharing with you what worked for me.

If you follow my advice in this book, you will never have to read another book about BPD, you will never have to watch another video about narcissism. You will never have to go onto another reddit forum about any of this craziness.

If you want to be free, do the ONE thing and then get on with your life.

OK, I think that's all I've got for now. If you want to hear me blather on for hours and hours about BPD and NPD abuse and the causes, go to my YouTube channel. There are hours and hours of videos with question and answer livestreams for your entertainment.

Or just do the ONE thing and move on with your life.

I wish you all the healing and joy that this world has to offer. May you find true happiness and love.

Mike

Printed in Great Britain
by Amazon